Editorial Project Manager
Lorin E. Klistoff, M.A.

Editor-in-Chief
Sharon Coan, M.S. Ed.

Cover Artist
Brenda DiAntonis

Art Coordinator
Kevin Barnes

Art Director
CJae Forshay

Imaging
Ralph Olmedo, Jr.
Rosa C. See

Product Manager
Phil Garcia

Publishers
Rachelle Cracchiolo, M.S. Ed.
Mary Dupuy Smith, M.S. Ed.

Dr. Fry's Word Sorts
Working with
Phonemes

Easy Consonants

Directions: Sort these pictures so that the /t/ pictures are under the monster and the other pictures are under the trash can.

Author

Edward Fry, Ph.D.

Teacher Created Materials

Teacher Created Materials, Inc.
6421 Industry Way
Westminster, CA 92683
www.teachercreated.com.
ISBN-0-7439-3712-0
©2003 Teacher Created Materials, Inc.
Made in U.S.A.

Table of Contents

Introduction

Preparing students for phonics is an important task! *Word Sorts: Working with Phonemes* is a great way for students to manipulate pictures, sounds, and words in a fun and meaningful way! The word sorts contained in this book are for the very beginning reader or early reader. They do not require any reading ability. However, the student who is an early reader can practice reading the words while he or she is sorting. Students may not know how to read all the words, but they will be expected to learn some phoneme awareness and some awareness of the fact that both single letters and digraphs (two-letter combinations) make speech sounds (phonemes). Included in this book are some digraphs that will help students prepare for more formal phonics lessons later. Many of these exercises require the student to hear the difference between sounds at the beginning of words and show the difference by sorting pictures that have similar sounds.

Note, however, that reading pictures is not quite as easy as it sounds, because one student might call a picture a "house" while another student might call the picture a "cabin" or "shack." Hence, for the exercises that show pictures, the teacher should read the words for each picture in the lesson so that the student will call the picture by the correct name. Specific phonics instructions are included at the top of these activity pages.

Other exercises do not use pictures because the sound (phoneme/grapheme correspondence) does not often occur at the beginning of a word, or there are no pictures to illustrate the sound. These exercises use written words. The phonics instructions are also included at the top of these pages.

These word sorts are by no means a complete beginning reading program. However, the word sorts are useful supplemental activities. The activities can be placed at a center. The word sorts can be done individually or in a group setting. The activities can also be used as a quick assessment of each student. In place of cutting the words out, the teacher may elect to have students mark the correct answers with a color. For example, the teacher may ask the students to color all the beginning *t* pictures yellow. It is highly recommended that in conjunction with these word sort activities, students hear stories being read aloud to them and have many opportunities to tell their own stories orally.

Easy Consonants

Phonics Instructions: The letter *t* is a consonant that usually makes the sound /t/, as in *top*. This sound can be made without using the vocal cords or schwa sound at the end. Say /t/, not "tuh." Ask the student to practice the /t/ sound in isolation. Then read aloud the name for each picture: ball, bed, top, train, frog, table, tree, mouse. Have the student sort the pictures.

Student Directions: Cut out the pictures at the bottom of the page. Place the pictures that begin with the /t/ sound under the letter *t*. Place the others under the trash can.

Easy Consonants

Phonics Instructions: The letter *n* is a consonant that usually makes the sound /n/, as in *no*. This sound always uses the vocal cords, but should not be followed by the schwa sound. Just say /n/, not "nuh." Ask the student to practice the /n/ sound in isolation. Then read aloud the name for each picture: nest, fish, nine, bat, ring, nurse, nickel, jam. Have the student sort the pictures.

Student Directions: Cut out the pictures at the bottom of the page. Place the pictures that begin with the /n/ sound under the letter *n*. Place the others under the trash can.

Easy Consonants

Pl___ Instructions: The letter *r* is a consonant that usually makes the /r/ sound, as in *red*. This sou___ ___ways uses the vocal cords, but should not be followed with a schwa at the end. Say /r/, not "ruh." Ask the student to practice the /r/ sound in isolation. Then read aloud the name for each picture: rabbit, fan, ruler, pig, rake, radio, lips, wagon. Have the student sort the pictures.

Student Directions: Cut out the pictures at the bottom of the page. Place the pictures that begin with the /r/ sound under the letter *r*. Place the others under the trash can.

Easy Consonants

Phonics Instructions: The letter *m* is a consonant that usually makes the /m/ sound, as in *man*. This sound always uses the vocal cords, but should not be followed with a schwa at the end. Say /m/, not "muh." Ask the student to practice the /m/ sound in isolation. Then read aloud the name for each picture: man, pencil, goat, moon, meat, mop, block, kite. Have the student sort the pictures.

Student Directions: Cut out the pictures at the bottom of the page. Place the pictures that begin with the /m/ sound under the letter *m*. Place the others under the trash can.

Easy Consonants

Phonics Instructions: The letter *d* is a consonant that usually makes the /d/ sound, as in *dog*. This sound always uses the vocal cords and the schwa, but do not overemphasize the schwa. Ask the student to practice the /d/ sound in isolation. Then read aloud the name for each picture: duck, car, frog, dress, wagon, mask, drum, dog. Have the student sort the pictures.

Student Directions: Cut out the pictures at the bottom of the page. Place the pictures that begin with the /d/ sound under the letter *d*. Place the others under the trash can.

8   © *Teacher Created Materials, Inc.*

Easy Consonants

Phonics Instructions: The letter *s* is one of the few consonants that has two sounds. The sound /s/, as in *saw*, is the most common. The letter *s* almost always makes this sound at the beginning of a word. This sound can be made without using the vocal cords or the schwa sound at the end. Say /s/, not "suh." Ask the student to practice the /s/ sound in isolation. Then read aloud the name for each picture: sun, watch, saw, cat, sock, star, pig, flower. Have the student sort the pictures.

Student Directions: Cut out the pictures at the bottom of the page. Place the pictures that begin with the /s/ sound under the letter *s*. Place the others under the trash can.

Easy Consonants

Phonics Instructions: The letter *l* is a consonant that usually makes the /l/ sound, as in *look*. This sound always uses the vocal cords but should not be followed with a schwa at the end. Say /l/, not "luh." Ask the student to practice the /l/ sound in isolation. Then read aloud the name of each picture: lamp, key, leaf, table, jar, ladder, letter, house. Have the student sort the pictures.

Student Directions: Cut out the pictures at the bottom of the page. Place the pictures that begin with the /l/ sound under the letter *l*. Place the others under the trash can.

Easy Consonants

Phonics Instructions: The letter *c* usually has the sound of /k/. For example, the *c* in the word *cat* has the sound of /k/. This sound can be made without using the vocal cords or the schwa sound at the end. The letter *c* usually makes the /k/ sound before *a*, *o*, and *u*. Ask the student to practice the /k/ sound in isolation. Then read aloud the name of each picture: cat, rug, vest, cup, ring, glove, car, cow. Have the student sort the pictures.

Student Directions: Cut out the pictures at the bottom of the page. Place the pictures that begin with the /k/ sound under the letter *c*. Place the others under the trash can.

Easy Consonants

Phonics Instructions: The letter *p* is a consonant that usually has the sound of /p/, as in *pig*. This sound can be made without using the vocal cords or the schwa sound at the end. Say /p/, not "puh." Ask the student to practice the /p/ sound in isolation. Then read aloud the name of each picture: pig, yarn, fire, pencil, paint, penny, brush, vase. Have the student sort the pictures.

Student Directions: Cut out the pictures at the bottom of the page. Place the pictures that begin with the /p/ sound under the letter *p*. Place the others under the trash can.

Easy Consonants

Phonics Instructions: The letter *b* is a consonant that makes the sound of /b/, as in *boy*. This sound uses the vocal cords and the schwa; however, do not overemphasize the schwa. Say /b/, not "buh." Ask the student to practice the /b/ sound in isolation. Then read aloud the name of each picture: book, snake, box, pie, bell, wig, mop, bowl. Have the student sort the pictures.

Student Directions: Cut out the pictures at the bottom of the page. Place the pictures that begin with the /b/ sound under the letter *b*. Place the others under the trash can.

Easy Consonants

Phonics Instructions: The letter *f* is a consonant that almost always makes the sound /f/, as in *fish*. This sound can be made without using the vocal cords or the schwa sound at the end. Say /f/, not "fuh." Ask the student to practice the /f/ sound in isolation. Then read aloud the name of each picture: fish, flower, pizza, bird, saw, fox, bag, fan. Have the student sort the pictures.

Student Directions: Cut out the pictures at the bottom of the page. Place the pictures that begin with the /f/ sound under the letter *f*. Place the others under the trash can.

Easy Consonants

Phonics Instructions: The letter *v* is a consonant that usually has the sound /v/, as in *very*. This sound always uses the vocal cords but should not be followed with a schwa at the end. Say /v/, not "vuh." Ask the student to practice the /v/ sound in isolation. Then read aloud the name of each picture: vest, comb, vase, shoe, cap, tire, van, violin. Have the student sort the pictures.

Student Directions: Cut out the pictures at the bottom of the page. Place the pictures that begin with the /v/ sound under the letter *v*. Place the others under the trash can.

Short Vowels

Phonics Instructions: The letter *a* is a vowel that has several sounds. The short sound of *a*, as in *as*, is the most common and should be taught first. Ask the student to practice the /a/ sound in isolation. Then read aloud the name of each picture: fish, apple, comb, ant, bell, alligator, wig, ax. Have the student sort the pictures.

Student Directions: Cut out the pictures at the bottom of the page. Place the pictures that begin with the short /a/ sound under the letter *a*. Place the others under the trash can.

Short Vowels

Phonics Instructions: The letter *e* is a vowel that has several sounds. The short sound of *e*, as in *end*, should be taught first, because it is the most common. Ask the student to practice the short /e/ in isolation. Then read aloud the name of each picture: elephant, moon, duck, eggs, cat, elbow, sun, elf. Have the student sort the pictures.

Student Directions: Cut out the pictures at the bottom of the page. Place the pictures that begin with the short /e/ sound under the letter *e*. Place the others under the trash can.

Short Vowels

Phonics Instructions: The letter *i* is a vowel that has several sounds. The short sound of *i*, as in *is*, should be taught first, because it is the most common. Ask the student to practice the short /i/ sound in isolation. Then read aloud the name of each picture: lamp, igloo, Indian, ball, insect, rake, ink, nurse. Have the student sort the pictures.

Student Directions: Cut out the pictures at the bottom of the page. Place the pictures that begin with the short /i/ sound under the letter *i*. Place the others under the trash can.

Short Vowels

Phonics Instructions: The letter *o* is a vowel that has several sounds. The short sound of *o*, as in *on*, is the most common and should be taught first. Ask the student to practice the short /o/ sound in isolation. Read the name of each picture: ostrich, key, otter, wig, fish, octopus, oxen, bell. Have the student sort the pictures.

Student Directions: Cut out the pictures at the bottom of the page. Place the pictures that begin with the short /o/ sound under the letter *o*. Place the others under the trash can.

Short Vowels

Phonics Instructions: The letter *u* is a vowel that has several sounds. The short sound of *u*, as in *up*, is the most common and should be taught first. Ask the student to practice the short /u/ sound in isolation. Read the name of each picture: umbrella, underwear, kite, fly, moon, undersea, vase, umpire. Have the student sort the pictures.

Student Directions: Cut out the pictures at the bottom of the page. Place the pictures that begin with the short /u/ sound under the letter *u*. Place the others under the trash can.

Common Exceptions

Phonics Instructions: The letter *y* is most frequently a vowel that has the long *e* sound, as in *very*. This is true when *y* is at the end of a word that contains another vowel. Ask the student to practice the long /e/ sound in isolation. Read the words on the page aloud with the student repeating them. Have the student sort the words.

Student Directions: Cut out the words at the bottom of the page. Place the words that begin with the long /e/ sound under the letter *y*. Place the others under the trash can.

baby | any | on | many

are | with | very | his

Common Exceptions

Phonics Instructions: The letter *e* at the end of the word that contains another vowel sound is usually silent. This rule is more useful and consistent than the Final "e" Rule, which will be taught later. Read the words aloud with the student repeating them. Have the student sort the words.

Student Directions: Cut out the words at the bottom of the page. Place the words that end with the silent *e* under the letter *e*. Place the others under the trash can.

one   were   at   be

this   or   there   come

Long Vowels (Final "e" Rule)

Phonics Instructions: The second most common sound of *a* is the long sound, as in *take*. The long *a* is frequently made by placing a silent *e* at the end of the word or syllable. Note the difference between *mad* and *made*. Ask the student to practice the long /ā/. Read aloud the words with the student repeating them. Have the student sort the words.

Student Directions: Cut out the words at the bottom of the page. Place the words with the long *a* sound together under the monster. Place the others under the trash can.

make   one   made   at

take   by   same   words

Long Vowels (Final "e" Rule)

Phonics Instruction: The second most common sound of *i* is the long sound, as in *like*. The long *i* sound is frequently made by placing a silent *e* at the end of a word. Ask the student to practice the long /ī/ sound in isolation. Read the words aloud with the student repeating them. Have the student sort the words.

Student Directions: Cut out the words at the bottom of the page. Place the words with the long *i* sound together under the monster. Place the others under the trash can.

five	but
not	line
what	in
side	write

Long Vowels (Final "e" Rule)

Phonics Instructions: The second most common sound of *o* is the long sound as in *home*. It is frequently made by placing a silent *e* at the end of the word or syllable. Ask the student to practice the long /ō/ sound in isolation. Read the words aloud with the student repeating them. Have the student sort the words.

Student Directions: Cut out the words at the bottom of the page. Place the words with the long *o* sound together under the monster. Place the others under the trash can.

o – e

| all | bone | were | not |
| home | hope | we | those |

Long Vowels (Open Syllable Rule)

Phonics Instructions: The long sound of *a* is sometimes made by the "Open Syllable Rule," which states that when a syllable ends in a vowel, the vowel is pronounced with the long sound, as in *paper*. Ask the student to practice the long /ā/ sound in isolation. Read the name of each picture: glue, bed, lady, baby, radio, gum, pig, table. Have the student sort the pictures.

Student Directions: Cut out the pictures at the bottom of the page. Place the pictures with the long *a* sound together under the monster. Place the others under the trash can.

Long Vowels (Open Syllable Rule)

Phonics Instructions: The long sound of *e* is sometimes made by the "Open Syllable Rule," which states that when a syllable ends in a vowel, the vowel is pronounced with the long sound, as in *me*. Ask the student to practice the long /ē/ sound in isolation. Then read the name of each picture: three, box, equal, cat, car, tree, lamp, beehive. Have the student sort the pictures.

Student Directions: Cut out the pictures at the bottom of the page. Place the pictures with the long *e* sound together under the monster. Place the others under the trash can.

Long Vowels (Open Syllable Rule)

Phonics Instructions: The long sound of *i* is sometimes made by the "Open Syllable Rule," which states that when a syllable ends in a vowel, the vowel is pronounced with the long sound, as in *tiger*. Ask the student to practice the long /ī/ sound in isolation. Then read the name of each picture: duck, tiger, triangle, flag, bicycle, spider, frog, book. Have the student sort the pictures.

Student Directions: Cut out the pictures at the bottom of the page. Place the pictures with the long *i* sound together under the monster. Place the others under the trash can.

Long Vowels (Open Syllable Rule)

Phonics Instructions: The long sound of *o* is sometimes made by the "Open Syllable Rule," which states that when a syllable ends in a vowel, the vowel is pronounced with the long sound, as in *go*. Ask the student to practice the long /ō/ sound in isolation. Then read the name of each picture: ocean, potato, bag, skate, piano, radio, net, scale. Have the student sort the pictures.

Student Directions: Cut out the pictures at the bottom of the page. Place the pictures with the long *o* sound together under the monster. Place the others under the trash can.

Long Vowels (Open Syllable Rule)

Phonics Instructions: The long sound of *u* is sometimes made by the "Open Syllable Rule," which states that when a syllable ends in a vowel, the vowel is pronounced with the long sound, as in *human*. Ask the student to practice the long /yo͞o/ sound in isolation. Then read the words aloud with the student repeating them. Have the student sort the words.

Student Directions: Cut out the words at the bottom of the page. Place the words with the long *u* sound together under the monster. Place the others under the trash can.

ruler | be | tuba | this

music | have | human | or

Difficult Consonants

Phonics Instructions: The consonant *g* has two sounds. The most common is the /g/ sound as in *good*. It frequently makes this sound before *a, o, u,* and when it is the last letter in a word. This sound uses the vocal cords and the schwa; however, do not overemphasize the schwa. Ask the student to practice the /g/ sound in isolation. Then read the name of each picture: grapes, glass, book, pencil, elephant, tire, gum, girl. Have the student sort the pictures.

Student Directions: Cut out the pictures at the bottom of the page. Place the pictures that begin with the /g/ sound under the letter *g*. Place the others under the trash can.

Difficult Consonants

Phonics Information: The letter *h* is a consonant that usually makes the /h/ sound, as in *hat*. This sound can be made without using the vocal cords or the schwa sound at the end. Say /h/, not "huh." Ask the student to practice the /h/ sound in isolation. Then read the name of each picture: box, horse, hand, tree, home, bat, car, hat. Have the student sort the pictures.

Student Directions: Cut out the pictures at the bottom of the page. Place the pictures that begin with the /h/ sound under the letter *h*. Place the others under the trash can.

Difficult Consonants

Phonics Instructions: The letter *k* is a consonant that usually makes the /k/ sound, as in *kind*. This sound can be made without using the vocal cords or the schwa sound at the end. Say /k/, not "kuh." Ask the student to practice the /k/ sound in isolation. Then read the name of each picture: key, frog, ring, kite, king, drum, jam, kangaroo. Have the student sort the pictures.

Student Directions: Cut out the pictures at the bottom of the page. Place the pictures that begin with the /k/ sound under the letter *k*. Place the others under the trash can.

Difficult Consonants

Phonics Instructions: The letter *w* is a consonant that usually makes the /w/ sound, as in *we*. This sound uses the vocal cords and the schwa. Do not overemphasize the schwa. Say /w/, not "wuh." Ask the student to practice the /w/ sound in isolation. Then read the name of each picture: pig, mask, woman, wagon, wig, watch, penny, fire. Have the student sort the pictures.

Student Directions: Cut out the pictures at the bottom of the page. Place the pictures that begin with the /w/ sound under the letter *w*. Place the others under the trash can.

Difficult Consonants

Phonics Instructions: The letter *j* is a consonant that usually makes the /j/ sound, as in *just*. This sound uses the vocal cords and the schwa. Do not overemphasize the schwa. Ask the student to practice the /j/ sound in isolation. Read the name of each picture: jam, jacket, duck, paint, table, mouse, jar, jacks. Have the student sort the pictures.

Student Directions: Cut out the pictures at the bottom of the page. Place the pictures that begin with the /j/ sound under the letter *j*. Place the others under the trash can.

Difficult Consonants

Phonics Instructions: The letter *x* does not have a sound of its own. The letter *x* usually sounds like /ks/, as in *box*. This sound can be made without using the vocal cords or the schwa sound at the end. The letter *x* is usually found at the end of a word or syllable. Ask the student to practice the /ks/ sound in isolation. Then read the name of each picture: yarn, dog, fox, six, box, ax, elephant, igloo. Have the student sort the pictures.

Student Directions: Cut out the pictures at the bottom of the page. Place the pictures that have the /ks/ sound under the letter *x*. Place the others under the trash can.

Difficult Consonants

Phonics Instructions: The letter *q* is a consonant of relatively low frequency. It always appears with *u*. The combination *qu* makes the /kw/ sound, as in *queen*. Ask the student to practice the /kw/ sound in isolation. Then read the name of each picture: rake, queen, quarter, question, top, quilt, fan, bed. Have the student sort the pictures.

Student Directions: Cut out the pictures at the bottom of the page. Place the pictures that begin with the /kw/ sound under the letters *qu*. Place the others under the trash can.

Difficult Consonants

Phonics Instructions: The letter *z* is a consonant that usually makes the /z/ sound, as in *zoo*. This sound always uses the vocal cords but should not be followed with a schwa at the end. Say /z/, not "zuh." Ask the student to practice the /z/ sound in isolation. Then read the name of each picture: zebra, zero, ring, penny, cup, table, zipper, zucchini. Have the student sort the pictures.

Student Directions: Cut out the pictures at the bottom of the page. Place the pictures that begin with the /z/ sound under the letter *z*. Place the others under the trash can.

Difficult Consonants

Phonics Instructions: When *y* is at the beginning of a word, it makes the /y/ sound, as in *yes*. This uses the vocal cords and the schwa; however, do not overemphasize the schwa. Say /y/, not "yuh." Ask the student to practice the /y/ sound in isolation. Then read the name of each picture: shoe, leaf, yarn, cap, yo-yo, yogurt, yacht, comb. Have the student sort the pictures.

Student Directions: Cut out the pictures at the bottom of the page. Place the pictures that begin with the /y/ sound under the letter *y*. Place the others under the trash can.

Consonant Digraphs

Phonics Instructons: *Th* is a consonant digraph that has two sounds, neither of which is a blend of *t* and *h*. This sound most frequently found in words commonly taught to beginning readers is the voiced *th*, as in *the*. Voiced means that the vocal cords are used in making the *th* sound. It can be made without the schwa sound at the end. Ask the student to practice the voiced /<u>th</u>/ sound in isolation. Then read the words aloud with the student repeating them. Have the student sort the words.

Student Directions: Cut out the words at the bottom of the page. Place the words that begin with the /<u>th</u>/ sound under the letters *th*. Place the others under the trash can.

Consonant Digraphs

Phonics Instructions: The voiceless *th*, as in the word *thin*, does not use the vocal cords. It can be made without the schwa sound at the end. Ask the student to practice the voiceless /th/ sound in isolation. Then read the name of each picture: thimble, cow, thread, vase, thirteen, pie, thumb, mop. Have the student sort the pictures.

Student Directions: Cut out the pictures at the bottom of the page. Place the pictures that begin with the /th/ sound under the letters *th*. Place the others under the trash can.

Consonant Digraphs

Phonics Instructions: The digraph *ch* makes the sound heard at the beginning of the word *child*. It is not a blend of *c* and *h*, but is a unique sound. This sound is voiceless and can be made without the schwa sound at the end. Ask the student to practice the /ch/ sound in isolation. Then read the name of each picture: chair, pencil, cheese, ladder, children, bird, cherries, snake. Have the student sort the pictures.

Student Directions: Cut out the pictures at the bottom of the page. Place the pictures that begin with the /ch/ sound under the letters *ch*. Place the others under the trash can.

Consonant Digraphs

Phonics Instructions: The digraph *sh* makes the sound heard at the beginning of the word *she*. It is not a blend of *s* and *h*, but is a unique sound. This sound is voiceless and can be made without the schwa sound at the end. Ask the student to practice the /sh/ sound in isolation. Then read the name of each picture: shirt, sheep, nickel, lamp, jar, violin, shell, shorts. Have the student sort the pictures.

Student Directions: Cut out the pictures at the bottom of the page. Place the pictures that begin with the /sh/ sound under the letters *sh*. Place the others under the trash can.

Consonant Digraphs

Phonics Instructions: The digraph *wh* makes the sound heard at the beginning of the word *when*. It is not a blend of *w* and *h*. It is a unique sound, usually called a consonant digraph, but sometimes referred to as the sound of *h* and *w* blended. This sound is voiceless and can be made without the schwa sound at the end. Ask the student to practice the /hw/ sound in isolation. Then read aloud the name of each picture: apple, book, king, wheel, whistle, whale, wheat, jacket. Have the student sort the pictures.

Student Directions: Cut out the pictures at the bottom of the page. Place the pictures that begin with the /hw/ sound under the letters *wh*. Place the others under the trash can.

Consonant Second Sounds

Phonics Instructions: The second sound of *c* is the /s/ sound, as in *city*. The letter *c* frequently makes this sound before *i*, *e*, and *y*. This sound can be made without using the vocal cords or the schwa sound at the end. Ask the student to practice the /s/ sound in isolation. Read aloud the words with the student repeating them. Have the student sort the pictures.

Student Directions: Cut out the words at the bottom of the page. Place the words that begin with the /s/ sound under the letter *c*. Place the others under the trash can.

cents   that   city   it

certain   he   century   for

Consonant Second Sounds

Phonics Instructions: The second sound of *s* is the /z/ sound as in *has*. The sound always uses the vocal cords, but should not be followed with a schwa at the end. The letter *s* tends to make the /z/ sound when it is the final sound in a word or syllable if it is preceded by a voiced sound. The letter *s* makes the /z/ sound in words much more frequently than *z* itself does. Therefore, the most common way to spell the /z/ sound is with *s*. Ask the student to practice making the /z/ sound in isolation. Then read aloud the words with the student repeating them. Have the student sort the words.

Student Directions: Cut out the words at the bottom of the page. Place the words that have the /z/ sound under the letter *s*. Place the others under the trash can.

s

| is | on | are | as |
| with | they | was | his |

Consonant Second Sounds

Phonics Instructions: The second sound of *g* is the /j/ sound, as in *general*. This /j/ sound of *g* is often made when *g* is followed by *i*, *e*, or *y*. This sound uses the vocal cords and the schwa; however, do not overemphasize the schwa. Ask the student to practice the /j/ sound in isolation. Read the words aloud with the student repeating them. Have the student sort the words.

Student Directions: Cut out the words at the bottom of the page. Place the words that have the /j/ sound under the letter *g*. Place the others under the trash can.

g

gym | giant | at | this

genie | germ | have | had

Consonant Second Sounds

Phonics Instructions: The letter *y* sometimes sounds like long *i*, as in *my*. This is usually when it is at the end of a word that contains no other vowel or when *y* appears in the middle of a word, as in *cyclone*. Ask the student to practice the long /ī/ in isolation. Then read the words aloud with the student repeating them. Have the student sort the words.

Student Directions: Cut out the words at the bottom of the page. Place the words that have the long /ī/ sound under the letter *y*. Place the others under the trash can.

| my | by | why | words |
| but | not | what | cry |

Schwa Sounds

Phonics Instructions: The schwa sound is the unaccented vowel sound like *a* in *ago*. It is the same sound whether it is made by *a* in *ago* or *o* in *of*. Some dictionaries say that the schwa sound and the short *u* sound are the same. The schwa sound has a fairly high frequency and is important for anyone using phonics. Ask the student to practice the schwa /ə/ sound in isolation. Then read the words aloud with the student repeating them. Have the student sort the words.

Student Directions: Cut out the words at the bottom of the page. Place the words that have the /ə/ sound under the letter *a*. Place the others under the trash can.

about   the   in   above

you   this   ago   again

Schwa Sounds

Phonics Instructions: The *schwa* sound is the unaccented vowel sound like *e* in *enough*. It is the same sound whether it is made by *a* in *ago*, *e* in *enough*, or *o* in *of*. The schwa sound has a fairly high frequency and is important for anyone using phonics. Ask the student to practice the schwa /∂/ sound in isolation. Then read the words aloud with the student repeating them. Have the student sort the words.

Student Directions: Cut out the words at the bottom of the page. Place the words that have the /∂/ sound under the letter *e*. Place the others under the trash can.

| silent | quiet | that | it |

| was | hundred | children | for |

Schwa Sounds

Phonics Instructions: The schwa sound is the unaccented vowel or short *u* like *o* in *come*. It is the same sound whether it is made by *a* in *ago* or *o* in *of*. The schwa sound has a fairly high frequency and is important for anyone using phonics. Ask the student to practice the schwa /ə/ in isolation. Read the words aloud with the student repeating them.

Student Directions: Cut out the words at the bottom of the page. Place the words that have the /ə/ sound under the letter o. Place the others under the trash can.

other | of | often | are

with | his | they | office

Long Vowel Digraphs

Phonics Instructions: The long *e* sound is sometimes made by the two-letter combination (digraph) *ea*, as in *eat*. This is sometimes referred to as the double vowel rule, but there are so many double vowels that do not make a long vowel sound that it is preferable to pick out only those which do and call them long vowel digraphs. Ask the student to practice the long /ē/ sound in isolation. Then read the words aloud with the student repeating them. Have the student sort the words.

Student Directions: Cut out the words at the bottom of the page. Place the words that have the long /ē/ sound under the letters *ea*. Place the others under the trash can.

each   at   eat   this

had   sea   it   read

Long Vowel Digraphs

Phonics Instructions: The long *e* sound is also made by the two-letter combination (digraph) *ee*, as in *three*. This is sometimes referred to as the double vowel, but there are so many double vowels that do not make a long vowel sound that it is preferable to pick out only those which do and call them long vowel digraphs. Ask the student to practice the long /ē/ sound in isolation. Then read the words aloud with the student repeating them. Have the student sort the words.

Student Directions: Cut out the words at the bottom of the page. Place the words that have the long /ē/ sound under the letters *ee*. Place the others under the trash can.

Long Vowel Digraphs

Phonics Instructions: The long *a* sound is sometimes made by the two-letter combination (digraph) *ai*, as in *rain*. This is sometimes referred to as the double vowel rule, but there are so many double vowels that do not make a long vowel sound that it is preferable to pick out only those which do and call them long vowel digraphs. Ask the student to practice the long /ā/ sound in isolation. Then read the words aloud with the student repeating them. Have the student sort the words.

Student Directions: Cut out the words at the bottom of the page. Place the words that have the long /ā/ sound under the letters *ai*. Place the others under the trash can.

Long Vowel Digraphs

Phonics Instructions: The long *a* sound is also made by the two-letter combination (digraph) *ay*, as in *day*. Ask the student to practice the long /ā/ sound in isolation. Then read the words aloud with the student repeating them. Have the student sort the words.

Student Directions: Cut out the words at the bottom of the page. Place the words that have the long /ā/ sound under the letters *ay*. Place the others under the trash can.

play the of day

say may and to

Long Vowel Digraphs

Phonics Instructions: The long *o* sound is sometimes made by the two-letter combination (digraph) *oa*, as in *coat*. This is sometimes referred to as the double vowel rule, but there are so many double vowels that do not make a long vowel sound that it is preferable to pick out only those which do and call them long vowel digraphs. Ask the student to practice the long /ō/ sound in isolation. Then read the words aloud with the student repeating them. Have the student sort the words.

Student Directions: Cut out the words at the bottom of the page. Place the words that have the long /ō/ sound under the letters *oa*. Place the others under the trash can.

Long Vowel Digraphs

Phonics Instructions: The long *o* sound is also sometimes made by the two-letter combination (digraph) *ow*, as in *show*. Ask the student to practice the long /ō/ sound in isolation. Then read the words aloud with the student repeating them. Have the student sort the words.

Student Directions: Cut out the words at the bottom of the page. Place the words that have the long /ō/ sound under the letters *ow*. Place the others under the trash can.

| own | it | slow | he |
| show | for | low | was |

Vowel Plus R

Phonics Instructions: The letter combination *or* makes the sound heard in *or* or *for*. Ask the student to practice the long /ôr/ sound in isolation. Then read the words aloud with the student repeating them. Have the student sort the words.

Student Directions: Cut out the words at the bottom of the page. Place the words that have the long /ôr/ sound under the letters *or*. Place the others under the trash can.

of

and

for

force

in

that

form

forest

Vowel Plus R

Phonics Instructions: The letter combination *ar* makes two sounds. The first sound is *ar*, as in *care*. It is a combination of short *e* /e/ plus *r* /r/. Ask the student to practice the /er/ sound in isolation. Then read the words aloud with the student repeating them. Have the student sort the words.

Student Directions: Cut out the words at the bottom of the page. Place the words that have the /er/ sound under the letters *ar*. Place the others under the trash can.

care   his   rare   share

aware   they   at   this

Vowel Plus R

Phonics Instructions: The letter combination *ar* makes two sounds. The second sound is /är/, as in *far*. Ask the student to practice the /är/ sound in isolation. Then read the words aloud with the student repeating them. Have the student sort the words.

Student Directions: Cut out the words at the bottom of the page. Place the words that have the /är/ sound under the letters *ar*. Place the others under the trash can.

car | it | art | he

far | with | arm | for

Vowel Plus R

Phonics Instructions: The letter combination *er* makes the sound by the *er* in *her*. It is a combination of short *u* /u/ plus *r* /r/. Ask the student to practice the /ər/ sound in isolation. Then read the words aloud with the student repeating them. Have the student sort the words.

Student Directions: Cut out the words at the bottom of the page. Place the words that have the /ər/ sound under the letters *er*. Place the others under the trash can.

her | have | over | or

after | had | water | by

Vowel Plus R

Phonics Instructions: The letter combination *ir* makes the sound made by the *ir* in *girl*. It is a combination of short *u* /u/ plus *r* /r/. Ask the student to practice the /∂r/ sound in isolation. Then read the words aloud with the student repeating them. Have the student sort the words.

Student Directions: Cut out the words at the bottom of the page. Place the words that have the /∂r/ sound under the letters *ir*. Place the others under the trash can.

girl   bird   but   not

first   in   that   sir

Vowel Plus R

Phonics Instructions: The letter combination *ur* makes the sound made by *ur* in *turn*. It is a combination of short *u* /u/ plus *r* /r/. Ask the student to practice the /ər/ sound in isolation. Then read the words aloud with the student repeating them. Have the student sort the words.

Student Directions: Cut out the words at the bottom of the page. Place the words that have the /ər/ sound under the letters *ur*. Place the others under the trash can.

| burn | but | church | fur |
| turn | not | in | all |

Broad O

Phonics Instructions: The broad *o* sound, as in *off*, is frequently made by the letter *o*. It is often made by *a* in combination with *l*, *u*, or *w*. Ask the student to practice the /ô/ sound in isolation. Then read the words aloud with the student repeating them. Have the student sort the words.

Student Directions: Cut out the words at the bottom of the page. Place the words that have the /ô/ sound under the letter *o*. Place the others under the trash can.

the

and

off

often

soft

long

in

that

64

Broad O

Phonics Instructions: The broad *o* sound, as in *off*, is frequently made by the letter *o*. It is also made by *a* in combination with *l*, *u*, or *w*. Ask the student to practice the /ôl/ sound in isolation. Then read the words aloud with the student repeating them. Have the student sort the words.

Student Directions: Cut out the words at the bottom of the page. Place the words that have the /ôl/ sound under the letters *al*. Place the others under the trash can.

al

always   also   it   already

he   was   for   all

Broad O

Phonics Instructions: The broad *o* sound is frequently made by *a* followed by *w*, as in *awful*. Ask the student to practice the /ô/ sound in isolation. Then read the words aloud with the student repeating them. Have the student sort the words.

Student Directions: Cut out the words at the bottom of the page. Place the words that have the /ô/ sound under the letters *aw*. Place the others under the trash can.

Broad O

Phonics Instructions: The broad *o* sound is also frequently made by *a* followed by *u*, as in *auto*. Ask the student to practice the /ô/ sound in isolation. Then read the words aloud with the student repeating them. Have the student sort the words.

Student Directions: Cut out the words at the bottom of the page. Place the words that have the /ô/ sound under the letters *au*. Place the others under the trash can.

they   at   cause   author

caught   autumn   be   this

Diphthongs

Phonics Instructions: The diphthong sound /ou/ is usually made by the letters *ou*, as in *out*. Ask the student to practice the /ou/ sound in isolation. Then read the words aloud with the student repeating them. Have the student sort the words.

Student Directions: Cut out the words at the bottom of the page. Place the words that have the /ou/ sound under the letters *ou*. Place the others under the trash can.

out   had   by   our

house   hour   have   it

Diphthongs

Phonics Instructions: The dipthong sound /ou/, as in *out*, is also made by *ow*, as in *cow*. Ask the student to practice the /ou/ sound in isolation. Then read the words aloud with the student repeating them. Have the student sort the words.

Student Directions: Cut out the words at the bottom of the page. Place the words that have the /ou/ sound under the letters *ow*. Place the others under the trash can.

OW

words | but | what | how

now | cows | down | all

Diphthongs

Phonics Instructions: The diphthong sound /oi/ is usually made by the letters *oi*, as *oil*. Ask the student to practice the /oi/ sound in isolation. Then read the words aloud with the student repeating them. Have the student sort the words.

Student Directions: Cut out the words at the bottom of the page. Place the words that have the /oi/ sound under the letters *oi*. Place the others under the trash can.

oi

oil   were   join   we

noise   when   point   you

70

Diphthongs

Phonics Instructions: The diphthong sound /oi/ is also made by *oy*, as in *boy*. Ask the student to practice the /oi/ sound in isolation. Then read the words aloud with the student repeating them. Have the student sort the words.

Student Directions: Cut out the words at the bottom of the page. Place the words that have the /oi/ sound under the letters *oy*. Place the others under the trash can.

boy   enjoy   the   toy

of   and   in   destroy

Difficult Vowels

Phonics Instructions: The letter combination *oo* has two sounds, as seen in the words *moon* and *book*. The so-called long sound, or two-dot *u* sound, as in *moon*, is the most common. Ask the student to practice the long /o͞o/ sound in isolation. Then read the words aloud with the student repeating them. Have the student sort the words.

Student Directions: Cut out the words at the bottom of the page. Place the words that have the long /o͞o/ sound under the letters *oo*. Place the others under the trash can.

moon | that | it | he

school | are | soon | room

72

Difficult Vowels

Phonics Instructions: The second sound of the letter combination *oo* is the so-called short *oo* or one-dot *u* sound, as in the word *look*. Ask the student to practice the short /ŏŏ/ sound in isolation. Then read the words aloud with the student repeating them. Have the student sort the words.

Student Directions: Cut out the words at the bottom of the page. Place the words that have the short /ŏŏ/ sound under the letters *oo*. Place the others under the trash can.

Difficult Vowels

Phonics Instructions: The sound of *u*, as in *rule*, is sometimes called the long *oo* or two-dot *u* sound and is the same sound made by *moon*. Ask the student to practice the long /$\overline{oo}$/ sound in isolation. Then read the words aloud with the student repeating them. Have the student sort the words.

Student Directions: Cut out the words at the bottom of the page. Place the words that have the long /$\overline{oo}$/ sound under the letter *u*. Place the others under the trash can.

| ruler | or | truth | had |
| flute | by | June | words |

Difficult Vowels

Phonics Instructions: The sound of *u*, as in *put*, is sometimes called the short *oo* or one-dot *u* sound, and is the same sound made by *oo* in *look*. Ask the student to practice the short /o͝o/ sound in isolation. Then read the words aloud with the student repeating them. Have the student sort the words.

Student Directions: Cut out the words at the bottom of the page. Place the words that have the short /o͝o/ sound under the letter *u*. Place the others under the trash can.

put   not   full   what

bush   all   were   pulled

Difficult Vowels

Phonics Instructions: The short *e* is sometimes made by the letter combination *ea*, as in *head*. Ask the student to practice the short /e/ sound in isolation. Then read the words aloud with the student repeating them. Have the student sort the words.

Student Directions: Cut out the words at the bottom of the page. Place the words that have the short /e/ sound under the letters *ea*. Place the others under the trash can.

head | dead | we | your

ahead | and | heavy | that

Beginning Consonant Blends

Phonics Instructions: The letter combination *bl* is a consonant blend of two consonant sounds. Ask the student to practice the /bl/ sound in isolation. Then read the name of each picture: blanket, jacket, block, dime, bleach, kite, blouse, zipper. Have the student sort the pictures.

Student Directions: Cut out the pictures at the bottom of the page. Place the pictures that have the /bl/ sound under the letters *bl*. Place the others under the trash can.

Beginning Consonant Blends

Phonics Instructions: The letter combination *cl* is a consonant blend of two consonant sounds. Ask the student to practice the /cl/ sound in isolation. Then read the name of each picture: gum, clock, mop, clothes, hat, cloud, zebra, clown. Have the student sort the pictures.

Student Directions: Cut out the pictures at the bottom of the page. Place the pictures that have the /cl/ sound under the letters *cl*. Place the others under the trash can.

Beginning Consonant Blends

Phonics Instructions: The letter combination *fl* is a consonant blend of two consonant sounds. Ask the student to practice the /fl/ sound in isolation. Then read the name of each picture: flower, flag, hand, horse, queen, kangaroo, flashlight, fly. Have the student sort the pictures.

Student Directions: Cut out the pictures at the bottom of the page. Place the pictures that have the /fl/ sound under the letters *fl*. Place the others under the trash can.

Beginning Consonant Blends

Phonics Instructions: The letter combination *gl* is a consonant blend of two consonant sounds. Ask the student to practice the /gl/ sound in isolation. Then read the name of each picture: glass, shell, globe, zipper, woman, glue, penny, glove. Have the student sort the pictures.

Student Directions: Cut out the pictures at the bottom of the page. Place the pictures that have the /gl/ sound under the letters *gl*. Place the others under the trash can.

80

Beginning Consonant Blends

Phonics Instructions: The letter combination *pl* is a consonant blend of two consonant sounds. Ask the student to practice the /pl/ sound in isolation. Then read the name of each picture: planets, plant, mop, gum, plate, plus, horse, tree. Have the student sort the pictures.

Student Directions: Cut out the pictures at the bottom of the page. Place the pictures that have the /pl/ sound under the letters *pl*. Place the others under the trash can.

Beginning Consonant Blends

Phonics Instructions: The letter combination *sl* is a consonant blend of two consonant sounds. Ask the student to practice the /sl/ sound in isolation. Then read the name of each picture: sled, queen, slippers, pie, slide, thread, sleep, jacket. Have the student sort the pictures.

Student Directions: Cut out the pictures at the bottom of the page. Place the pictures that have the /sl/ sound under the letters *sl*. Place the others under the trash can.

Beginning Consonant Blends

Phonics Instructions: The letter combination *br* is a consonant blend of two consonant sounds. Ask the student to practice the /br/ sound in isolation. Then read the name of each picture: fan, elephant, bread, broom, brush, bridge, fly, cup. Have the student sort the pictures.

Student Directions: Cut out the pictures at the bottom of the page. Place the pictures that have the /br/ sound under the letters *br*. Place the others under the trash can.

Beginning Consonant Blends

Phonics Instructions: The letter combination *cr* is a consonant blend of two consonant sounds. Ask the student to practice the /cr/ sound in isolation. Then read the name of each picture: yacht, crayons, crown, glass, cracker, book, dog, crab. Have the student sort the pictures.

Student Directions: Cut out the pictures at the bottom of the page. Place the pictures that have the /cr/ sound under the letters *cr*. Place the others under the trash can.

Beginning Consonant Blends

Phonics Instructions: The letter combination *dr* is a consonant blend of two consonant sounds. Ask the student to practice the /dr/ sound in isolation. Then read the name of each picture: lamp, fish, drum, drink, comb, drill, dress, key. Have the student sort the pictures.

Student Directions: Cut out the pictures at the bottom of the page. Place the pictures that have the /dr/ sound under the letters *dr*. Place the others under the trash can.

Beginning Consonant Blends

Phonics Instructions: The letter combination *gr* is a consonant blend of two consonant sounds. Ask the student to practice the /gr/ sound in isolation. Then read the name of each picture: grass, nickel, grasshopper, bell, grapes, grandma, bed, sun. Have the student sort the pictures.

Student Directions: Cut out the pictures at the bottom of the page. Place the pictures that have the /gr/ sound under the letters *gr*. Place the others under the trash can.

Beginning Consonant Blends

Phonics Instructions: The letter combination *pr* is a consonant blend of two consonant sounds. Ask the student to practice the /pr/ sound in isolation. Then read the name of each picture: bag, princess, pray, yarn, prize, kite, top, present. Have the student sort the pictures.

Student Directions: Cut out the pictures at the bottom of the page. Place the pictures that have the /pr/ sound under the letters *pr*. Place the others under the trash can.

Beginning Consonant Blends

Phonics Instructions: The letter combination *tr* is a consonant blend of two consonant sounds. Ask the student to practice the /tr/ sound in isolation. Then read the name of each picture: tree, ball, pizza, train, truck, eggs, lamp, treasure. Have the student sort the pictures.

Student Directions: Cut out the pictures at the bottom of the page. Place the pictures that have the /tr/ sound under the letters *tr*. Place the others under the trash can.

Beginning Consonant Blends

Phonics Instructions: The letter combination *sc* is a consonant blend of two consonant sounds. Ask the student to practice the /sk/ sound in isolation. Then read the name of each picture: comb, scarf, scorpion, book, vase, screw, scale, jar. Have the student sort the pictures.

Student Directions: Cut out the pictures at the bottom of the page. Place the pictures that have the /sk/ sound under the letters *sc*. Place the others under the trash can.

Beginning Consonant Blends

Phonics Instructions: The letter combination *sk* is a consonant blend of two consonant sounds. Ask the student to practice the /sk/ sound in isolation. Then read the name of each picture: net, log, hat, skirt, skis, skunk, skate, duck. Have the student sort the pictures.

Student Directions: Cut out the pictures at the bottom of the page. Place the pictures that have the /sk/ sound under the letters *sk*. Place the others under the trash can.

90 © Teacher Created Materials, Inc.

Beginning Consonant Blends

Phonics Instructions: The letter combination *sn* is a consonant blend of two consonant sounds. Ask the student to practice the /sn/ sound in isolation. Then read the name of each picture: fire, vest, snowflake, snake, pie, snail, snorkel, yarn. Have the student sort the pictures.

Student Directions: Cut out the pictures at the bottom of the page. Place the pictures that have the /sn/ sound under the letters *sn*. Place the others under the trash can.

Beginning Consonant Blends

Phonics Instructions: The letter combination *sp* is a consonant blend of two consonant sounds. Ask the student to practice the /sp/ sound in isolation. Then read the name of each picture: sponge, tie, spoon, cat, elephant, spaceship, bike, spatula. Have the student sort the pictures.

Student Directions: Cut out the pictures at the bottom of the page. Place the pictures that have the /sp/ sound under the letters *sp*. Place the others under the trash can.

Beginning Consonant Blends

Phonics Instructions: The letter combination *st* is a consonant blend of two consonant sounds. Ask the student to practice the /st/ sound in isolation. Then read the name of each picture: stamp, star, monkey, block, doll, strawberry, boat, stapler. Have the student sort the pictures.

Student Directions: Cut out the pictures at the bottom of the page. Place the pictures that have the /st/ sound under the letters *st*. Place the others under the trash can.

Beginning Consonant Blends

Phonics Instructions: The letter combination *sw* is a consonant blend of two consonant sounds. Ask the student to practice the /sw/ sound in isolation. Then read the name of each picture: bat, sweater, rat, nest, frog, swing, swan, swim. Have the student sort the pictures.

Student Directions: Cut out the pictures at the bottom of the page. Place the pictures that have the /sw/ sound under the letters *sw*. Place the others under the trash can.

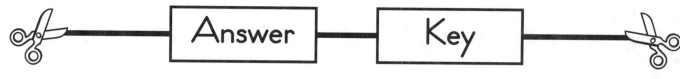

Page 4
t: top, train, table, tree
trash: ball, bed, frog, mouse
Page 5
n: nest, 9, nurse, nickel
trash: fish, bat, ring, jam
Page 6
r: rabbit, ruler, rake, radio
trash: fan, pig, lips, wagon
Page 7
m: man, moon, meat, mop
trash: pencil, goat, block, kite
Page 8
d: duck, dress, drum, dog
trash: car, frog, wagon, mask
Page 9
s: sun, saw, sock, star
trash: watch, cat, pig, flower
Page 10
l: lamp, leaf, ladder, letter
trash: key, table, jar, house
Page 11
c: cat, cup, car, cow
trash: rug, vest, ring, glove
Page 12
p: pig, pencil, paint, penny
trash: yarn, fire, brush, vase
Page 13
b: book, box, bell, bowl
trash: snake, pie, wig, mop
Page 14
f: fish, flower, fox, fan
trash: pizza, bird, saw, bag
Page 15
v: vest, vase, van, violin
trash: comb, shoe, cap, tire
Page 16
a: apple, ant, alligator, ax
trash: fish, comb, bell, wig
Page 17
e: elephant, eggs, elbow, elf
trash: moon, duck, cat, sun
Page 18
i: igloo, Indian, insect, ink
trash: lamp, ball, rake, nurse
Page 19
o: ostrich, otter, octopus, oxen
trash: key, wig, fish, bell

Page 20
u: umbrella, underwear, undersea, umpire
trash: kite, fly, moon, vase
Page 21
–y: baby, any, many, very
trash: on, are, with, his
Page 22
–e: one, were, there, come
trash: at, be, this, or
Page 23
a–e: make, made, take, same
trash: one, at, by, words
Page 24
i–e: five, line, side, write
trash: but, not, what, in
Page 25
o–e: bone, home, hope, those
trash: all, were, not, we
Page 26
a: lady, baby, radio, table
trash: glue, bed, gum, pig
Page 27
e: three, equal, tree, beehive
trash: box, cat, car, lamp
Page 28
i: tiger, triangle, bicycle, spider
trash: duck, flag, frog, book
Page 29
o: ocean, potato, piano, radio
trash: bag, skate, net, scale
Page 30
u: ruler, tuba, music, human
trash: be, this, have, or
Page 31
g: grapes, glass, gum, girl
trash: book, pencil, elephant, tire
Page 32
h: horse, hand, home, hat
trash: box, tree, bat, car
Page 33
k: key, kite, king, kangaroo
trash: frog, ring, drum, jam
Page 34
w: woman, wagon, wig, watch
trash: pig, mask, penny, fire
Page 35
j: jam, jacket, jar, jacks
trash: duck, paint, table, mouse

Page 36
x: fox, 6, box, ax
trash: yarn, dog, elephant, igloo
Page 37
qu: queen, quarter, question, quilt
trash: rake, top, fan, bed
Page 38
z: zebra, 0, zipper, zucchini
trash: ring, penny, cup, table
Page 39
y: yarn, yo-yo, yogurt, yacht
trash: shoe, leaf, cap, comb
Page 40
th: that, they, this, there
trash: of, and, to, you
Page 41
th: thimble, thread, 13, thumb
trash: cow, vase, pie, mop
Page 42
ch: chair, cheese, children, cherries
trash: pencil, ladder, bird, snake
Page 43
sh: shirt, sheep, shell, shorts
trash: nickel, lamp, jar, violin
Page 44
wh: wheel, whistle, whale, wheat
trash: apple, book, king, jacket
Page 45
c: cents, city, certain, century
trash: that, it, he, for
Page 46
s: is, as, was, his
trash: on, are, with, they
Page 47
g: gym, giant, genie, germ
trash: at, this, have, had
Page 48
y: my, by, why, cry
trash: words, but, not, what
Page 49
a: about, above, ago, again
trash: the, in, you, this
Page 50
e: silent, quiet, hundred, children
trash: that, it, was, for

Answer Key

Page 51

o: other, of, often, office
trash: are, with, his, they

Page 52

ea: each, eat, sea, read
trash: at, this, had, it

Page 53

ee: need, see, tree, three
trash: by, words, but, of

Page 54

ai: wait, paint, train, main
trash: not, what, were, me

Page 55

ay: play, day, say, may
trash: the, of, and, to

Page 56

oa: boat, road, coat, soap
trash: in, is, you, that

Page 57

ow: own, slow, show, low
trash: it, he, for, was

Page 58

or: for, force, form, forest
trash: of, and, in, that

Page 59

ar: care, rare, share, aware
trash: his, they, at, this

Page 60

ar: car, art, far, arm
trash: it, he, with, for

Page 61

er: her, over, after, water
trash: have, or, had, by

Page 62

ir: girl, bird, first, sir
trash: but, not, in, that

Page 63

ur: burn, church, fur, turn
trash: but, not, in, all

Page 64

o: off, often, soft, long
trash: the, and, in, that

Page 65

al: always, also, already, all
trash: it, he, was, for

Page 66

aw: saw, law, draw, straw
trash: on, ate, with, his

Page 67

au: cause, author, caught, autumn
trash: they, at, be, this

Page 68

ou: out, our, house, hour
trash: had, by, have, it

Page 69

ow: how, now, cows, down
trash: words, but, what, all

Page 70

oi: oil, join, noise, point
trash: were, we, when, you

Page 71

oy: boy, enjoy, toy, destroy
trash: the, of, and, in

Page 72

oo: moon, school, soon, room
trash: that, it, he, are

Page 73

oo: book, look, foot, good
trash: was, for, are, as

Page 74

u: ruler, truth, flute, June
trash: or, had, by, words

Page 75

u: put, full, bush, pulled
trash: not, what, all, were

Page 76

ea: head, dead, ahead, heavy
trash: we, your, and, that

Page 77

bl: blanket, block, bleach, blouse
trash: jacket, dime, kite, zipper

Page 78

cl: clock, clothes, cloud, clown
trash: gum, mop, hat, zebra

Page 79

fl: flower, flag, flashlight, fly
trash: hand, horse, queen,
  kangaroo

Page 80

gl: glass, globe, glue, glove
trash: shell, zipper, woman, penny

Page 81

pl: planets, plant, plate, plus
trash: mop, gum, horse, tree

Page 82

sl: sled, slippers, slide, sleep
trash: queen, pie, thread, jacket

Page 83

br: bread, broom, brush, bridge
trash: fan, elephant, fly, cup

Page 84

cr: crayons, crown, cracker, crab
trash: yacht, glass, book, dog

Page 85

dr: drum, drink, drill, dress
trash: lamp, fish, comb, key

Page 86

gr: grass, grasshopper, grapes,
  grandma
trash: nickel, bell, bed, sun

Page 87

pr: princess, pray, prize, present
trash: bag, yarn, kite, top

Page 88

tr: tree, train, truck, treasure
trash: ball, pizza, eggs, lamp

Page 89

sc: scarf, scorpion, screw, scale
trash: comb, book, vase, jar

Page 90

sk: skirt, skis, skunk, skate
trash: net, log, hat, duck

Page 91

sn: snowflake, snake, snail, snorkel
trash: fire, vest, pie, yarn

Page 92

sp: sponge, spoon, spaceship,
  spatula
trash: tie, cat, elephant, bike

Page 93

st: stamp, star, strawberry, stapler
trash: monkey, block, doll, boat

Page 94

sw: sweater, swing, swan, swim
trash: bat, rat, nest, frog